lovesick

janii yazon

BookLeaf Publishing

India | USA | UK

Presentation by *BookLeaf Publishing*

Web: www.bookleafpub.com

E-mail: info@bookleafpub.com

ISBN: 9789363305618

First edition 2024

for eve

ACKNOWLEDGEMENT

thank you to my family and friends, to oscar wilde and pablo neruda, to lang leav and anne carson, to people i've loved and places i've lived.

daring

i've never known what it's like
to feel the warmth of the sun
and the warmth of your touch
at the same time. instead,
like waves you wash over me
only when the moon is high,
and the heat of your breath
and my breath blowing under
blankets keeps the midnight
chill at bay.

your hand in my hand,
your nose in my neck –
i sweat the same as if it were
mid-july and i were pressed to
the shoulders of strangers on
the train. i flush the same as if
i fell asleep by the ocean, the end
of my nose tender, red to the touch.

how can they bear it? i find myself
wondering when just one warmth
is enough to burn me. and yet, still,
i yearn for it – me, with the crown
of my head growing hot in the day
and my palm growing sweaty against
the hem of your skirt.

where the light has gone

i want to rip the moon from its seat
and crush it between my palms,
wash the marble clean of my blood
and pierce its crater, hanged
off a simple chain

i want to brush your split ends off
your back and leave fingerprints
on the sweat of your nape and
seal the necklace shut

i want to pluck the stars and melt
them, mold them, press them into
the dust of your ceiling. i want to
convince the sun to come quietly,
sit in front of our living room tv

i want to hear the prophets announce
the end of the world, wonder where
the light has gone while our bed
drinks in muted starlight, a sitcom laugh-
track sneaks up through our floor,
and i kiss goodnight the moon-
carved shadow on your chest

avoidance

is my love for you that strong?
that i would move my life back
to the winter coast, to the land
of all i ran from — the bedroom
walls that never fade and the
aching hum of bathroom vents,
the silent starry evenings and
still silent mornings and silent
afternoons—if only to keep that
city the one where i held you
and our love sleeps peaceful
and smiles sweet, moves lazy
in our arms as morning starts
the birdsongs and brings your
whispers home?

romanticism

this is not a love poem. i did not love you
in the way quarter-sized paperbacks
fall off shelves or midday movies show
kisses in slow motion. i did not love you
like soft-strummed guitars sit in fireside
laps or sonnets conclude in neatly wrapped
couplets.
              instead, i loved you
in the way english poets rejected
the logical, in the face of all reason
and machine, and clutched the mess
of humanness between nail and palm
and stood before the world tragically
small in stature and knew pain was as
beautiful as love because it was as
human. that is how i loved you. like the
significance of all that i am and all that
i can be stared back at me and fear sat
right at home beside joy.

confession

you ask what i write about —
but it's you, it's always you.
moments with you fill these pages,
pictures of you spread out,
like this paper were a bed,
like these lines are shadows of half-
open blinds, patterns on your skin,
pen strokes long like farewell kisses.
nothing, even your name signed in ink,
could make the image of you any clearer.

memory

there, in the bedroom, is you
how i'd like to remember —
a shy smile and your eyes
dewy with the morning light
leaning through the window,
the angle soft over the
curve of your cheeks and the tip
of your nose. the memory of you
beneath the blankets and the un-
fulfilled wish to embrace you
carries me to sleep every night
and brings tears to my waking
eyes when the dream has dis-
sipated into the cold on
your side of the bed.

reflecting

and i think the ones who loved me
loved me like a painting
you see once and sit with.
you lean in close to read the label.
maybe google the artist or listen
to the pre-recorded explanation.
and maybe it means something
to you. you understand it, you
connect. you see its charm,
its merit.

and when you go home, maybe
you remember it. maybe you
write the name down somewhere
in the margins beside that poem
you think could make you a poet.

and when you go out, maybe
you talk about it. a filler fact to cushion
the corners in your conversation.
and maybe they want to know more,
but all you can say is, "i don't know,
i'll have to research them more but
it was really cool. oh! did you see…"

and when you forget, certainly,
the content of that painting fades
from memory and in its place is
the remembrance of a decent day.
the relief when you let your aching feet
rest and took a seat. a moment
you reflected on yourself.

beat fast, my heart

beat fast, my heart.
let summer rays run down
your sides like hands laying
claim and gasp and gasp
and hold love's ear
against your trembling chest —

let her listen to the sound
of unbearable longing and kiss
the thunder into humming,

learn the tune of storm-damp
dew and weave your arms up and up
to sigh a warm sigh into sunlit crowns,

and smile that mid-july smile
that splits your face, bright as lightning
and twice as rare

affirmations

i do not always wish i were gone.
there are moments laced with gold
i can recall, where the sun felt
like it should and laughter came
easily. there are moments soft
with lamplight and hands in mine
that quicken my heartbeat with
simple remembrance. there are
moments loud and fast where
bodies rush around mine and i
feel part of the swarm. there are
moments i look at the ink between
skin and bone, the line of my chest,
the morning mess of my hair, and shake
hands with my beauty. there are moments
i feel the ache of my tear-tapped eyes
and recognize this pain, like most, has passed.
i do not always wish i were gone.

weeds

should flowers bloom
simply because we bid
them so?

as dandelion seeds fog the
rabbits' view and speak an omen
to nearly trimmed grass,

i dream of flying weightless,
arms stretched to the sun,
the inhale before a breeze
urging me on.

to land where i land
and root where i root
and know only my spot
and be glad.

(and when spring returns
and i have passed my bloom,
i dream of the grace
to surrender once more to
nature's breath -- arms stretched
to the sun.)

circulation

i struggle to carry
the weight of my own heart
it sinks to my heels
crushed with each step
blue with bruises
and in my blood's
rush to feed the bleed,
my fingertips turn numb
and it feels like i still
have someone else
to wipe my tears

i hold my hands over
my chest and imagine
this is intimacy.

desire

i want to write my mind
on this page and recognize it.

i want to map the pulse
of my heart and know my way around.

i want to draw the curves
of my stomach, my nose,
and find them beautiful.

i want to lay bare
on these lines, weightless,
known.

the judgment of my parents
and their expectations do not
weigh on my shoulders.
instead, they lay tucked
beneath this box spring mattress
stained from immaturity. almost
imperceptible bumps that press
migraines behind my ears
and fatten the pockets between
my spine that pop in the after-
noon when i wake from
uneventful sleep – for rest
i need not dreams but quiet,
escape the future-past that
festers in the shadows
below me.

apology

i am sorry
but i am not sure what for.
all i know is that
my apologies are never alone.
they connect and spill like water
down these quivering lips,
mixing with eye-borne
saltwater, cheek-bound.

maybe i am sorry for that.

before love

Hesitation tastes sweet, like
thought of lips; the air between
my fingers warm as your hand must be.
I watch hope's vein pulse in time
with my own quiet thrum.

How many years I yearned to meet you
where rivers flow uphill under star-
snuck light to the tops of these forests,
in sheets of island wind, branches reach.

May I ask you, summer dawn, to wait
for us to touch? And from wet coqui
a simple song to push youth's restraint
aside? For in midyear heat, all is long,
and love lays too at ease.

memoria

i had almost forgotten
the scent of moonlight
when the wind
in its endless wish
to rest stopped
for breath against my
sunken cheeks and
in valediction drew out
my tears and
through the deluge i saw
written in the trees
the dirt's lush-hidden plea --
        remember

habits

i have seen leaves sleepwalk
off cloud-bound branches to curl
and clear into the earth or called
by keen breeze to leave

impressions of warmth in whorls
of red, of orange, of yellow against
lake-mirror skies, feigned depth of blue,
and walked away

the habits of new england
stay unimportant to me—
its unimpressive tired cyclicity

the undressing of trees
warned of the tunnels of night
winter drags against horizons
but still i stayed
searching for sorrowless times

until the nights became
ages lost to epochs.

temptation

breathe in, moon, the light of los angeles
rising like morning mist in the dead of night,
donning desires that cannot be put to sleep.

the post-thought foliage of palm trees
digests fluorescence and buzz; to the pulse
of evening traffic, ocean waves wax and wane.

watch dress suits ride the angels' flight
with one-dollar offerings and bow their heads.
the camera-flash flicker bursts in time with star
song.

breathe in, moon, sweet obsolescence.
listen to the flood tide sing aimless harmony
to desert breeze and retire to the shadow of
clouds.